I0110991

learning exploring discovering learning e… …ing discovering learning exploring discovering learning exploring discovering

Spain

Children's travel activity and keepsake book

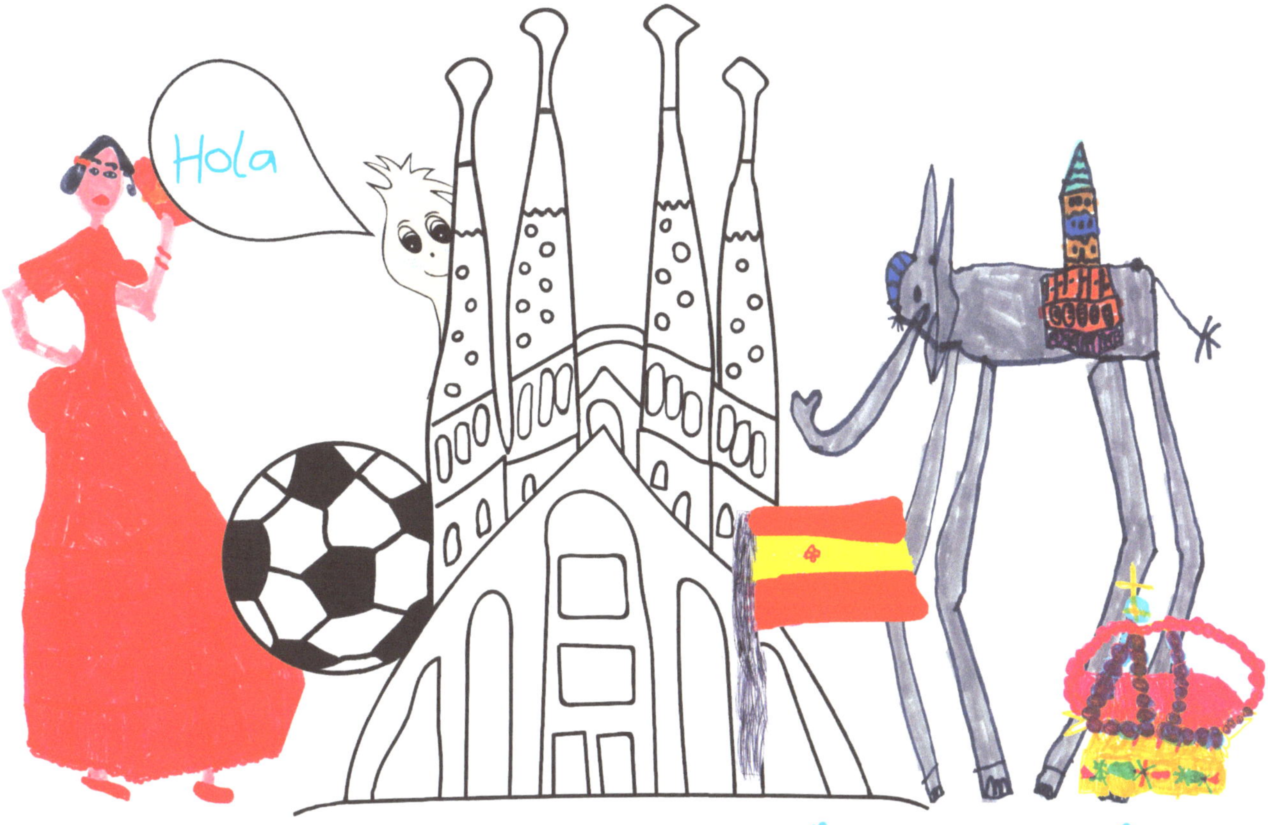

tinytourists
explore discover learn

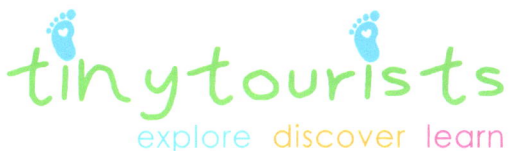

Hola !

Hello! My name's Topher*
and I love adventures!

I'll be keeping you company on your journey through this book. Look out for me, I'll be popping up every now and again.

Each time you see me say "Hola" to say hello

Count how many times you can spot me too...

*****Topher** is named after St. Chris**topher**, the patron saint for travellers who is known for keeping all those who travel safe from harm.

tinytourists is all about inspiring family travel and making the most of adventures; keeping travel meaningful and memorable, educational and fun. Visit us on Facebook to find out more and to join the tinytourists' community.

• •

Written and Designed by Louise Amodio
Illustrated by Louise Amodio and Catherine Mantle
Cover Illustrations by Luca (age 7), Emma (age 5), Francesca (age 8) and Greta (age 7).

Published by Beans and Joy Publishing Ltd as a product from Tiny Tourists Ltd, Great Britain.
www.tinytourists.co.uk

© Copyright 2016 Louise Amodio
All rights reserved. No part of this publication may be reproduced, stored in a retrieval system or transmitted in any means without the prior written permission of the Publisher.

ISBN: 978-0-9954949-4-7

This belongs to:

Design your own suitcase

Your adventure starts here

How to use this book

Welcome to your fun-packed travel activity book!

Look out for these symbols to tell you what type of activity you'll be doing so you can start to work independently:

 for writing and mark-making

 for drawing and colouring and being creative

Time to get started!

For the grown-ups to read:

Section 1: My Travel Log
Use this section to start thinking about your trip to Spain; when you're going, where you're going, who you're going with, what the weather be like, and what you'll pack in your suitcase. This will help form part of a lovely keepsake as well as practice your planning and organisational skills!

Section 2: Explorer Skills
This section is full of games and activities for a bit of Spain-themed fun. All are designed to support the National Curriculum and grouped into **Maths (p12-25), Literacy (p26-36), and The World Around Us (p37-42)**. See index for more details.

Also included are some spanish words you might like to try out during your trip. We give you the true spelling, the phoentic spelling (what it sounds like), and the english translation to make things straightforward.

phrase: hola
say: (ola)
meaning: hello

phrase: gracias
say: (grath-ius)
meaning: thank you

phrase: por favor
say: (poor fav-or)
meaning: please

Section 3: Memory Bank
This is where you can record all the memories from your trip. The perfect finishing touch to a lovely book of holiday memories; what you did, what you ate, what you saw, what you collected, and fun lists for recording the best bits and the worst bits.

Happy Travels!

My Travel Log

Me:

Stick or draw your picture here

My Destination:

Arrival:

Date: _____

Passport Stamp:

Departure:

Date: _____

Where am I going?

This is a map of Spain and her islands.
The capital city of Spain is Madrid - can you spot it?

Find out where you are going on holiday, any journeys you may be taking, and add them to the map:

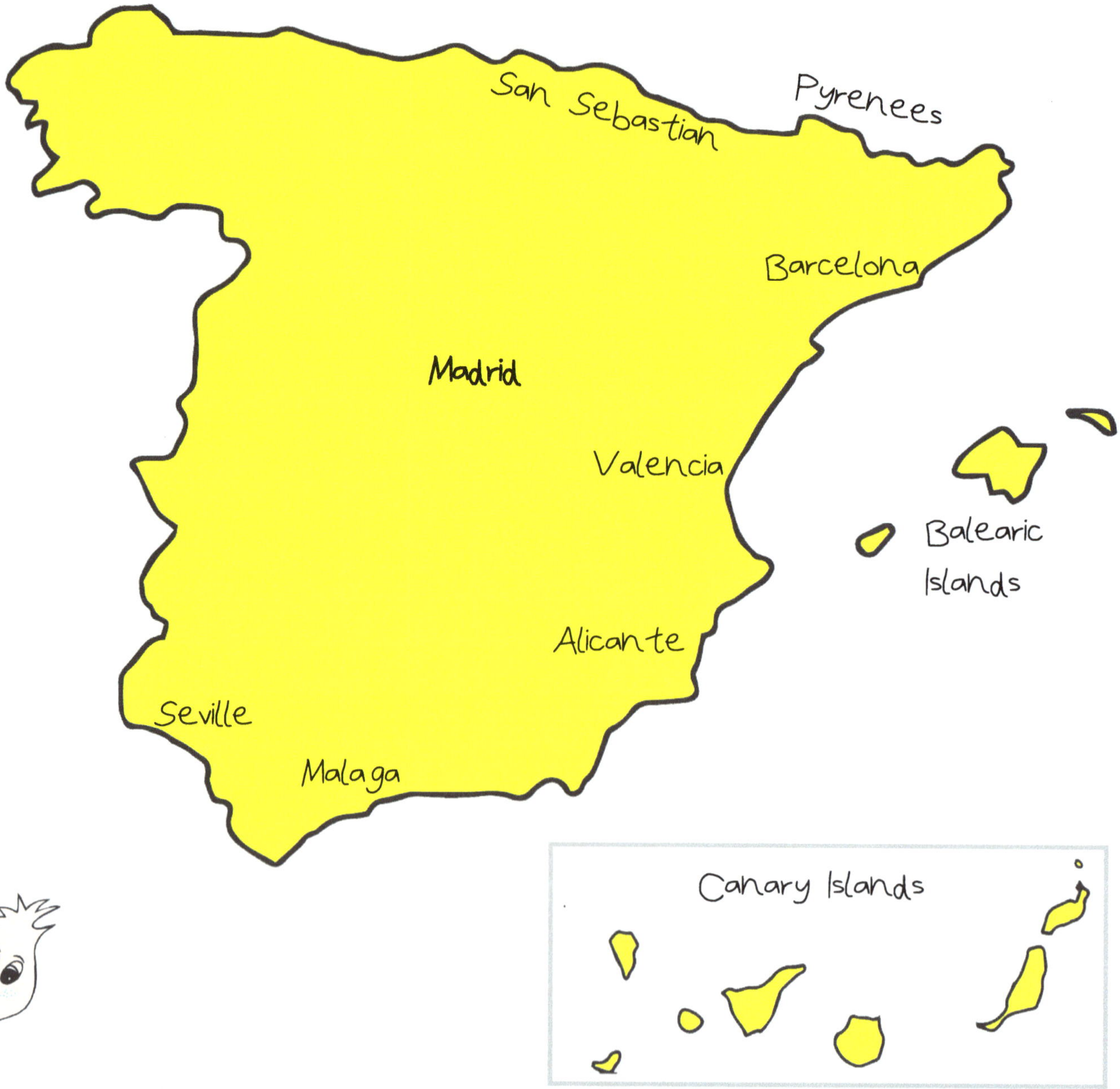

- San Sebastian
- Pyrenees
- Barcelona
- Madrid
- Valencia
- Balearic Islands
- Alicante
- Seville
- Malaga
- Canary Islands

How will I get there?

Find the transport you're using to get to Spain and colour it in:

Who am I going with?

Draw a picture of who you're going on holiday with in the frame below:

Example

Holiday Portrait

Mi mama
(mee mamar)
My mummy

Mi papa
(mee papar)
My daddy

Mi hermano
(mee ermano)
My brother

Mi hermana
(mee ermana)
My sister

# What will the weather be like?

Draw a circle around the weather you think you'll have:

esta lloviendo
(esta yoviendo)
It's raining

Esta soleado
(esta soli-ado)
It's sunny

Esta noviando
(esta noviando)
It's snowing

Explorer Skills

Problem-solving (Maths)   Communicating (Literacy)   Investigating (The World Around Us)

La Rojigualda

This is the Spanish flag, with yellow and red and the coat of arms.

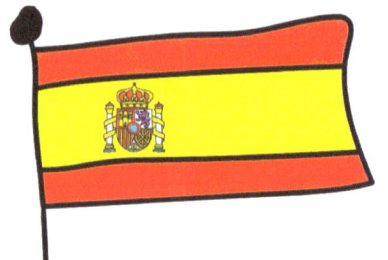

Complete the flag below by **adding the red and yellow stripes:**

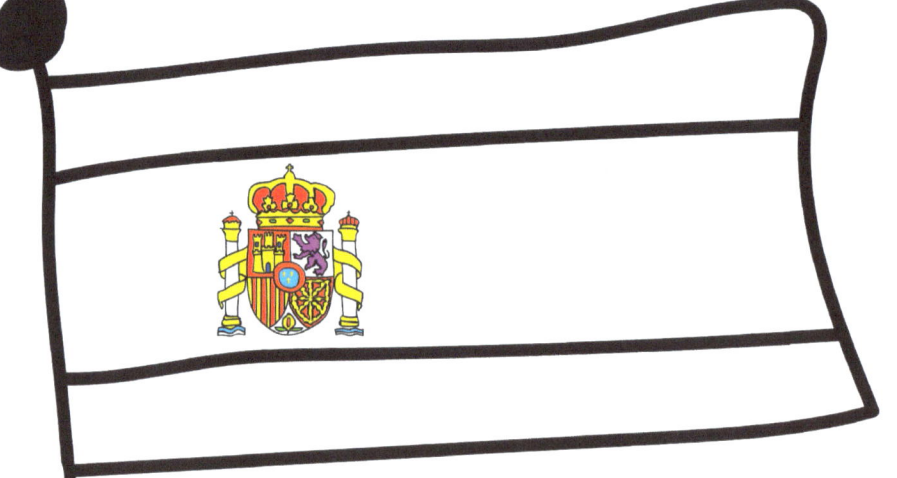

rojo
(roho)
red

amarillo
(amaree-o)
yellow

Red Flamenco Dancers

Flamenco is a style of Spanish dancing that involves singing, handclapping, foot stamping and finger-snapping. Can you do these things?

Circle all the flamenco dancers in **red** dresses. How many are there?

 # Yellow Flamenco Dancers

Circle all the flamenco dancers in **yellow** dresses.
How many are there?

# Design your own Flamenco dress

What are your favourite colours?
Design the Flamenco dress below in your own choice of colours:

Counting Food 1-5

Spain enjoys the perfect weather to grow juicy red tomatoes, fresh green olives, and bright and tangy oranges and lemons.

Count the fruit and vegetables below and circle the right number on the number line:

1 2 3 4 5   1 2 3 4 5

tomate
(tomatay)
tomato

aceituna
(avi-tuna)
olive

1 2 3 4 5   1 2 3 4 5

naranjas
(narran-has)
oranges

limon
(lee-mon)
lemon

Counting Food 1-10

Count the food and circle the right number below.
Which one do you think is your favourite?
Do you think this food is healthy or not healthy?

   1 2 3 4 5 6 7 8 9 10

   1 2 3 4 5 6 7 8 9 10

   1 2 3 4 5 6 7 8 9 10

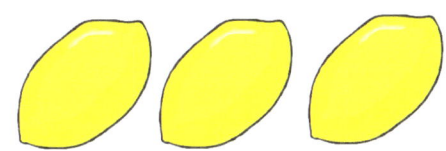   1 2 3 4 5 6 7 8 9 10

uno	dos	tres	cuatro	cinco	seis	siete	ocho	nueve	diez
oono	doz	trez	quadro	sinco	says	si-etay	ocho	noo-evay	dee-eth
1	2	3	4	5	6	7	8	9	10

Counting Seafood 1-5

As Spain has many beaches and many islands, food caught from the sea is very popular.

Count the prawns, lobster, fish and octopus below and circle the right number on the number line:

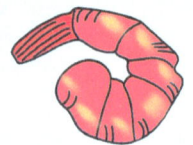

1 2 3 4 5

1 2 3 4 5

langostinos
(langosteen-os)
prawns

una langosta
(oona langosta)
a lobster

1 2 3 4 5

1 2 3 4 5

el pescado
(el peskardoe)
a fish

un pulpo
(oon pulpo)
an octopus

Counting Seafood 1-10

Count these foods and circle the right number below.

Have you tried any of these? Which is your favourite?

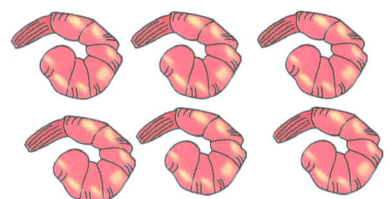
1 2 3 4 5 6 7 8 9 10

1 2 3 4 5 6 7 8 9 10

1 2 3 4 5 6 7 8 9 10

1 2 3 4 5 6 7 8 9 10

uno	dos	tres	cuatro	cinco	seis	siete	ocho	nueve	diez
oono	doz	trez	quadro	sinco	says	si-etay	ocho	noo-evay	dee-eth
1	2	3	4	5	6	7	8	9	10

Paella!

Paella is a popular dish in Spain. Its main ingredient is rice. Often prawns and mussels are added, and lemon juice is squeezed on top.

Can you **draw some ingredients** in this paella dish?

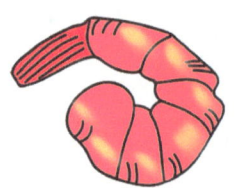

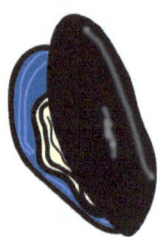

Matching Pairs - under the sea

Can you help these sea creatures find their friends?
Draw a line between each matching pair below.

Islands and Shells

Spain has two main groups of islands away from the mainland; the Canaries and the Balearics. All have sandy beaches to enjoy, and you might be lucky and spot some shells!

See if you can **find the smallest** shell on this sandy island:

Smallest Shell

Circle the **smallest** shell on each of these rows:

pequena
(peck-en-ya)
small

cascara
(caskara)
shell

Sunbathing!

Spain is often very sunny and people like to sunbathe on the sandy beaches. You might need a parasol to stop the sun from burning your skin.

Can you **find the biggest** parasol on this island?

Biggest Parasol

Circle the **biggest** parasol on each of these rows:

grande
(grond-ey)
big

sombrilla
(sombreeya)
parasol

Camp Nou

This huge football stadium is home to Barcelona Football Club. It's the biggest football stadium in Europe and some of the world's greatest football players have played here.

Use your colouring pencils to **add some colour** to this picture. The pitch is green, and the seating is red and blue.

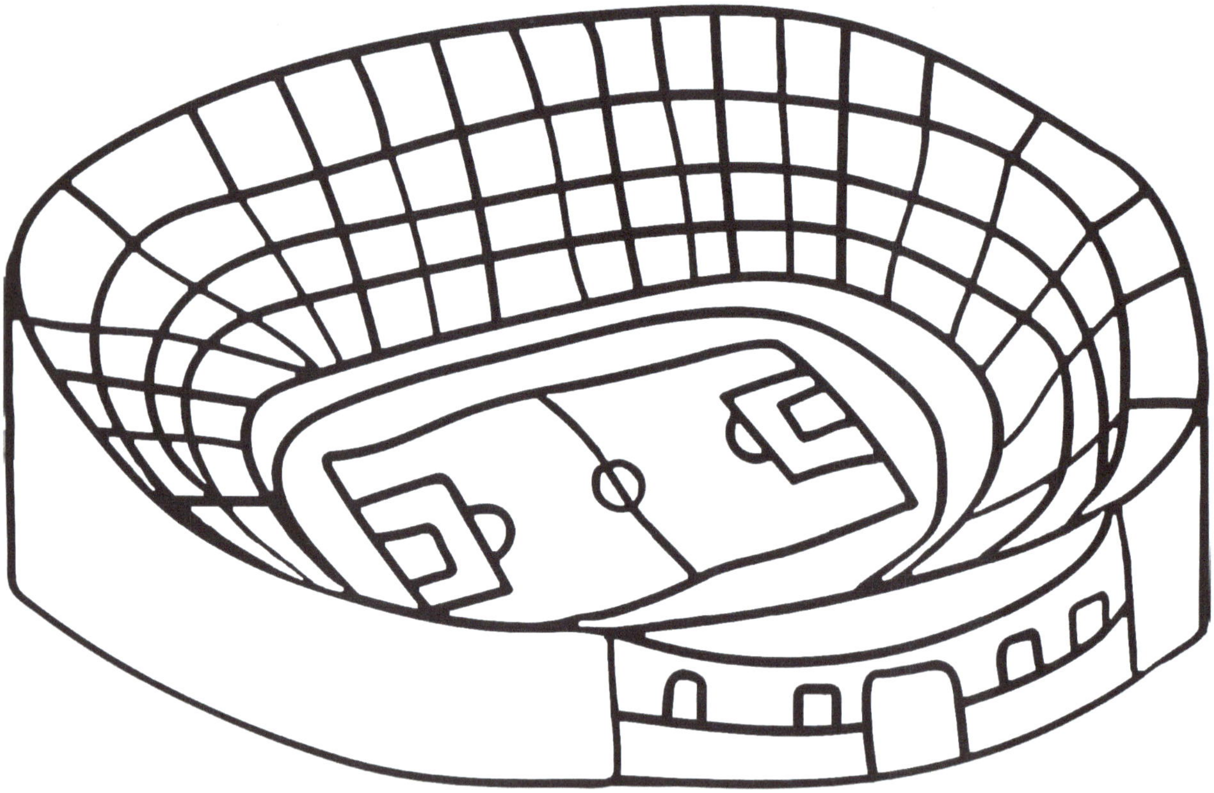

Sagrada Familia

In Barcelona, stands the Sagrada Familia - a weird and wonderful Cathedral designed by a man called Antoni Gaudi. It started to be built over 100 years ago and it still isn't finished yet!

Use your colouring pencils to **add some colour** to this picture. Add as many different colours as you can!

Football!

Spain's national sport is Football *(Futbol)* and has many fans. The Spanish football team wear red shirts.

Help score a goal - **guide this football through the maze** to the goal post:

Futbol !

Can you **trace along the dotted lines** between the balls and the goal posts to score some more goals?

Grand Prix

Spain hosts the Formula One car race in Barcelona, and has a history of successful racing car drivers too.

Can you **trace your way** through the maze to help the racing car reach the flags at the finishing line?

Circuit de Catalunya

The Spanish Grand Prix circuit is called the Circuit de Catalunya.

Can you **draw between the lines** showing the route around the track from start to finish?

coche de carreras
(cochay de carreras)
racing car

La Tomatina

In a small town in Spain, near Valencia, there is a huge tomato food fight every year on the last Wednesday of August. Over-ripe tomatoes are delivered and everyone throws them at each other!

What do you think these two people will look like at the end of the big tomato fight?

Add a splash of colour

Colour this picture matching the colours opposite, or in your own choice of colours.

Would you like to have a tomato fight one-day?

Shape-search

Find the objects in this grid that look like circles, ovals and semi-circles. How many are there of each?
Do you recognise any other shapes?

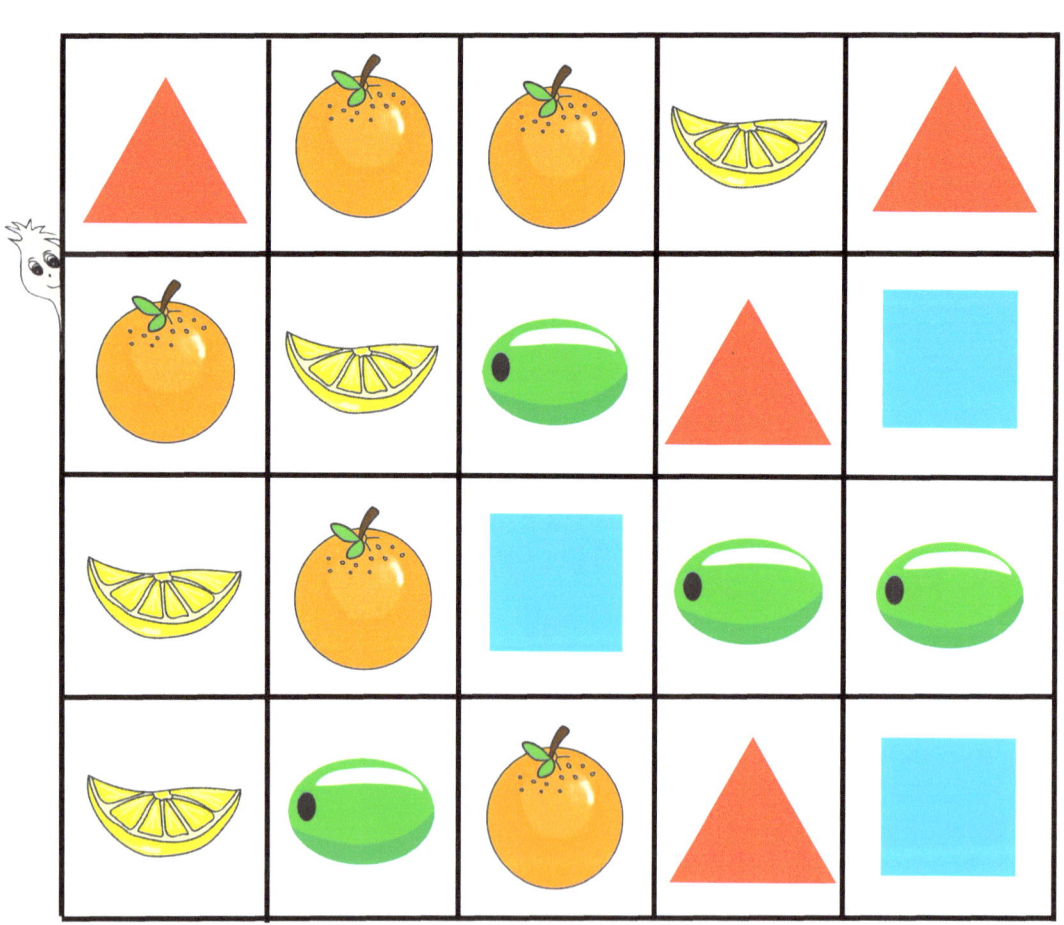

Letter-search - Spain

Find as many of these 3 letters in the grid as you can:

s _ p _ n _

s	n	n	i	s
t	p	s	p	i
s	s	a	n	s
n	n	p	s	t

Palazzo Reale di Madrid

Spain has a royal family with a king, queen and two princesses. Their official palace is the Palazzo Reale in Madrid.

Can you add some doors and windows to this castle, and add some of the royal family that live there?

What do you think they do when they're here?

Princesa
(printhesa)
princess

Principe
(printhe-pe)
prince

Finding the difference

Look along each row below and see if you can **find the castle that is different** to the others:

castillo
(castiyo)
castle

A Royal Spot the Difference

See if you can **spot the 5 differences** between these two crowns:

A Place to Stay

Where are you staying on your holiday in Spain? Is it a hotel? A house? A tent? A boat? A campervan? An apartment?

Can you **draw a picture** of it here?

Home Sweet Home

Can you **draw a picture** of where you live back at home?

What is different about this and your holiday home?

# What do you know about Spain?

Can you circle some of the things you might see in Spain?
Which things do you think you might NOT see?

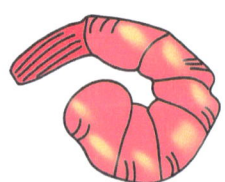

Memory Bank

Use this section to record and remember all the things you've done, seen and tasted on your trip!

Draw, Write, Staple, Stick!

You may need a grown up to help with some of the writing...

What have you eaten?

Draw some food you have eaten on holiday on the plate below. What was your favourite?

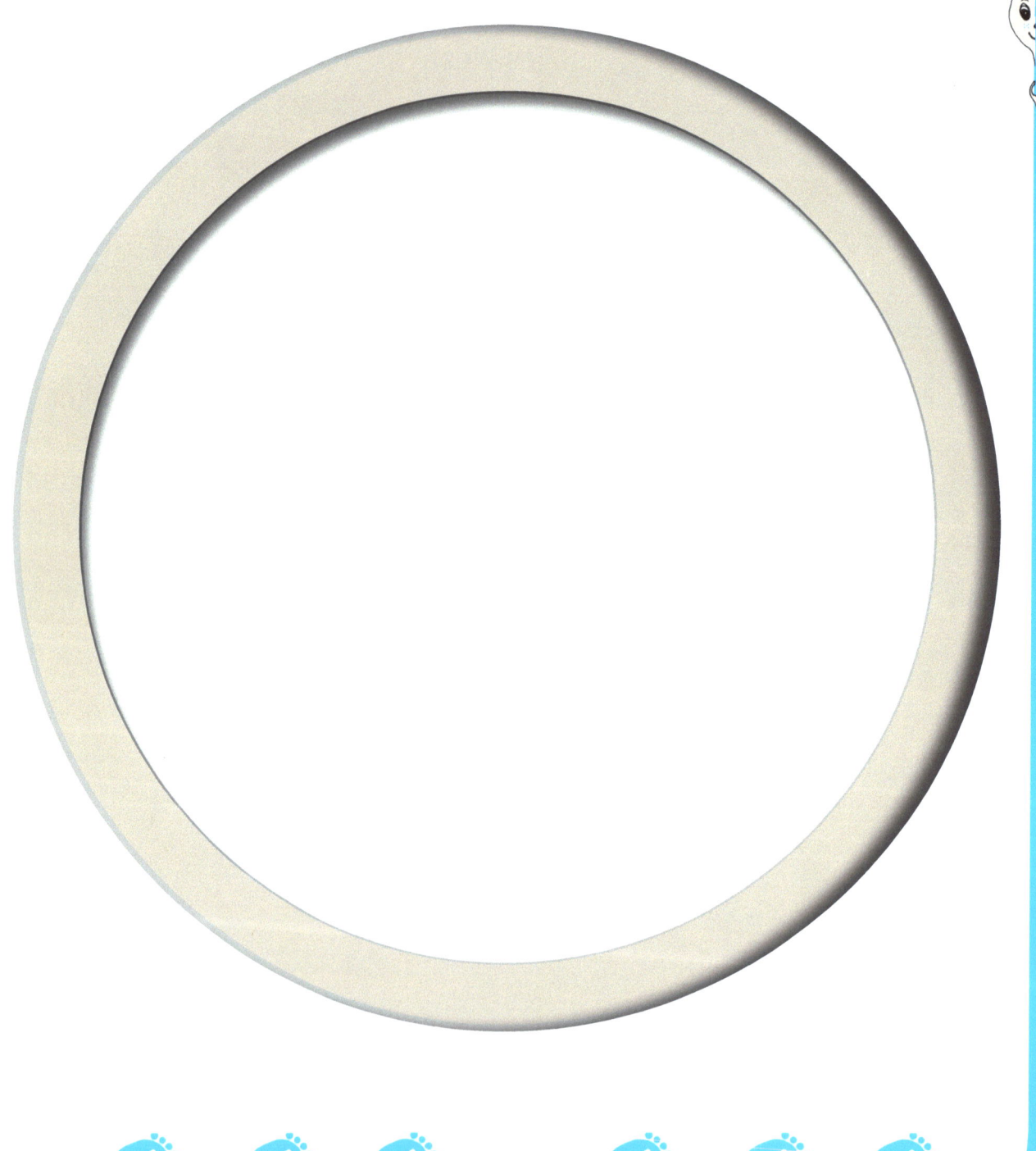

What adventures have you had?

Ask someone to help you **write a postcard** about your adventures, and design a nice stamp:

Tarjeta Postal

Momento Collage

Stick bits and pieces on these pages that you've collected during your trip; favourite tickets, receipts, leaflets, drawings, flowers...

Daily Diary

Note down some of the different things you have done each day:

Monday

Tuesday

Wednesday

Thursday

Friday

Saturday

Sunday

Memory Gallery

Draw pictures or doodles of any special memories:

Worst 5

What have been the **worst** five things about your trip?

_____

_____

_____

_____

_____

Top 5

What have been the **best** five things about your trip?

Index
(what's in this book and where you can find it)

Learning about Spain

Map of Spain	6
Spanish Flag	12
Spanish Dance - Flamenco	13-15
Spanish Food - Fruit, Vegetables, Seafood, Paella	16-21
Islands	22-25
Landmarks - Camp Nou and Sagrada Famiglia	26-27
Sports - Football and Formula One Racing	28-31
Festivals - La Tomatina	32-33
Spanish Royalty - Palaces and Castles	36-39

Supporting Key Skills

Mark-making and writing practice	13-14, 16-19, 22-25, 28-31, 45, 48
Observation and comparing	21, 22-25, 37-41
Colours and creativity	12-15, 20, 26-27, 33, 36
Shape and letter recognition	34-35
Counting and number recognition	16-19, 34-35
Storytelling; reflecting, re-counting, and guessing what happens next	32-33, 36, 44-45
Size; biggest and smallest	22-25
Planning and organising	6-10
Family	9
Days of the week	48
Language skills	8-10, 12, 16-19, 23, 25, 31, 37

Memory Making

	44-51

Adios
(goodbye)

I hope you enjoyed your adventure and completing this book along the way.

How many times did you spot me?

_____

Keep safe!
Love from
Topher xx

Where would you like to go next?

Italy · USA · Greece

France · Egypt · China

UK · Australia · South Africa

Thailand · Mexico · Finland